If You Can't Pay Attention, Take Notes

*A Navy Brat Reflects on Bratdom,
the First Line of Defense,
and Why You Don't Wash
the Chief's Coffee Cups*

Shelia Hempton Watson

**with her Dad,
RMC (Ret.) John Hempton, Jr.**

Tidal Creek Press
Charleston, South Carolina

TIDAL CREEK PRESS
A Division of Tidal Creek Productions LLC
PO Box 80983
Charleston, SC 29416
www.TidalCreekProductions.com
www.TidalCreekPress.com

Copyright © 2016 Shelia Hempton Watson

All rights reserved. No part of this book may be reproduced or used in any manner without written permission of the copyright owner except for the use of quotations in a book review. For more information, address: swatson@tidalcreekproductions.com

ISBN: 978-0-578-45819-9 (paperback)
ISBN: 978-0-578-45821-2 (ebook)

Some names and identifying details have been changed to protect the privacy of individuals.

Cover Photo Copyright © by Anthony Watson

For more information about the author
and other published works by the author,
visit **www.tidalcreekproductions.com**.

Dedication

For my father, who taught me diligence, work ethic, and perseverance.

And for my mother, who taught me that laughing at everything is the best way to live.

Acknowledgment

First let me state that I am a big fan of the U.S. military. They are the best, most powerful force on Earth, and all Armed Forces members, active duty and retired, deserve our respect.

That being said—with all sincerity and gratitude—I think the military, especially the Navy, has to admit that there are moments in the sailor's or brat's life that are just plain hilarious.

That's what we offer here: no disrespect intended, but full acknowledgment that parts of the military life—for both personnel and dependents—can be a bit of a giggle-fest.

If You Can't Pay Attention, Take Notes...

... when you start a story 1

... when advancing in the Navy is just one damn thing after another. 5

... when the unit you're in is the first to arrive on shore even before the Marines and the Seals 19

... when you get reminded that they didn't issue you a family with your seabag 23

... when most of your job requires staying on the good side of your detailer 29

... when training for war includes knowing how to play poker and pinochle. 43

... when Robert Mitchum stops by for a few beers 51

... when you spend an hour dressing up to meet the ship at Pier Papa . . . 55

... when you commandeer a jeep from
   the Army and it's too much
   paperwork for them to claim it 59

... when you're mistaken for NIS
   simply because you commute
   to the ship via helicopter 65

... when you have to dun the mob
   for $375. 69

... when SecNav sends a helicopter
   to deliver a gold-plated fishing
   rod to you 81

... when a fishing buddy turns out to be
   an undercover agent with NIS 87

... when your career is the least interesting
   thing about NAVFAC duty 93

... when you deserve hazard pay for
   rescuing Oscar 101

... when retirement looks suspiciously
   like active duty. 103

... when you have one more story
   to tell. 109

If you can't pay attention, take notes...

...when you start a story

There's an old saying that the difference between a fairy tale and a sea story is that a fairy tale starts off with "Once upon a time" and a sea story starts off with "This is no shit."

Let's just say that what follows is not a fairy tale.

Okay, it's also "no shit" in the strictest Navy sense.

That's not to say they're all *sea* stories. In fact, many of the stories involve shore duty or incidents that have nothing to do with being at sea.

But they're still sea stories in the

broadest sense of the term—that is to say, a glimpse of life in the Navy, sometimes with a hilarious ending (usually) or a vague moral (usually not) or profanity (almost always).

I should point out that these stories are Dad's recollections, with some selective editing and a few embellishments from me—and my point of view is in *italic* type.

The sharp memory and funny storytelling belongs to him; any errors are solely mine.

Keep that in mind as you browse through. Aside from the occasional embellished detail, these stories are most definitely *no shit*.

~ ~ ~

Dad never meant to go into the Navy. His original intention was to go into the Marine Corps Reserves, but when he went to talk to the recruiters, the Marine recruiting office was closed.

The Navy recruiting office next door was open, though, so he went in and, because the man had never met a stranger, he got into a conversation with the guy in there.

Before you could sing one verse of "Anchors Aweigh," he was signed up.

Which means I grew up a Navy brat instead of a Marine brat, and that was the least of the differences in the two paths.

Had he gone into the Marine Corps, no telling where I'd have grown up—San Diego, probably, or Beaufort, assuming he ended up as a drill sergeant.

I don't know, it's a weird possibility to contemplate. He doesn't really have the bellowing voice for a drill sergeant. And his wavy dark hair just wouldn't work with the Marine buzz-cut.

No, I think the Marine recruiting office being closed was a propitious stroke of luck. He was destined for the Navy. And it was destined for him.

If you can't pay attention, take notes...

... when advancing in the Navy is just one damn thing after another

Dad enlisted in the middle of his senior year in high school and went to boot camp during Christmas break when he was still seventeen.

Unfortunately for the Southern born and bred youngster, boot camp was in Great Lakes, Illinois. The weather nearly did him in, because ... well, I'll let him tell the story:

When I took off from Charleston, it was 70 degrees. By the time we landed in Chicago, it was 18 degrees. My pea coat was in the bottom of my sea bag because I didn't need it before I left. I just about froze to death.

Because I was scheduled to do the rest of my boot camp one night a week at the Charleston base, I only had to make it through two weeks, but it was the coldest two weeks of my life. I found out that Chicago lives up to its name of the windy city. No matter which way you go, the wind is blowing right in your face.

A few things stand out about boot camp. One was the wheel book (a small notebook) the drill instructor gave us and told us—in the loudest voice I ever heard in my life—how important it was:

"Pay attention to everything I say! And if for some reason you can't pay attention, take notes!"

Another thing that stood out was the firefighting drill we had to master. Like a lot of people back home on

Johns Island, I was a volunteer firefighter, and I knew that you were supposed to shut the hose off before handing it off to someone else. But in Great Lakes, it was so cold that if we shut the hose off, it froze and we'd have to take it down into a basement and thaw it. We learned pretty fast to throttle it down instead of shutting it off.

The other thing that comes to mind is the time three of us were assigned to clean the chiefs' barracks. One of the chiefs was sleeping because he had the night watch, so we just swept and mopped around him, and all was well.

Then we had to get out this huge buffer to finish up. When we plugged it in, it started running wild and vibrating like crazy. It was vibrating so much that it knocked the chief out the bunk. We finally got it unplugged, but the chief jumped up and started screaming at us. Then we had to go stand outside in the freezing cold until he finished sleeping. One of the guys in the cleaning crew complained to our drill instructor about having to wait for the chief to finish his nap, but the instructor just shrugged it off and said, "If you don't learn anything else in boot camp, you'd better learn this: Whatever the chief wants, the chief gets. And you better not ever wash his coffee cup."

We thought that was odd, but we found out later that leaving the chief's coffee cup alone was no joke. They said that when you start a cruise, the coffee in the cup that day starts the seasoning. Supposedly it has something to do with keeping the taste of home with you. But the bottom line is that if you interrupt the seasoning of the cup, there WILL be hell to pay.

Dad learned the lesson. Not only did he remember to be properly deferential to chiefs, but he recognized that chief was the thing to be. He found out soon enough that the old saying "it's the chiefs who run the Navy" wasn't just talk.

As a civilian, Dad had worked after school, on weekends, and during the summer as a pipefitter, so he aimed for shipfitting in the Navy.

And the Navy, with all the military logic it could muster, naturally assigned him to a completely different field from his skill set.

After those first couple of weeks in Great Lakes, the rest of boot camp involved me serving one night a week at the Charleston Naval Base.

By the time I went on active duty, I had finished all of boot camp and had advanced to seaman apprentice. I was stationed at the receiving station in Charleston waiting for orders, and while I waited, they had me update my information.

One of the things I took in school was typing, so I let them know that. I didn't realize it at the time, but that threw up a red flag because they had a critical need for radiomen. They immediately sent me to test to read Morse code. I thought that was a strange skill for a shipfitter, but it was the Navy. And that meant I had to do it. The Navy's always sending you to a school to learn something.

They started with the easiest letters: E, I, and T. E is one dot (called "dit"), I is two dots, and T is one dash (called "dah"). I put on earphones and listened to Morse code and a translation of which letter it was.

Dit. "That's E." Dit. "That's E."

Dit dit. "That's I." Dit dit. "That's I."

Dah. "That's T." Dah. "That's T."

It wasn't hard, but it was monotonous. Just "dits" and "dahs" all day, day after day. Fifty of us were in there, and by the time we were done, they selected ten. I was one of them.

A week later they told me I was being sent to RM school in Bainbridge, Maryland.

At that point I still thought I was going to end up being a shipfitter, and I had no idea what RM school was. When I got to Bainbridge, I found out it was radioman school. Then I found out how seriously they take different rates and divisions.

On the first day of school, the instructor called me to the front of the class and told me I was out of uniform. I looked down. I had on the right shirt, pants, and shoes. I didn't know what he was talking about.

Then he pointed to the red stripes on my sleeve. Those stripes designated below decks in the engine room, and it was what I'd been given when I enlisted.

"You're not a pipefitter anymore," he said. "You're a radioman striker. Get those red stripes off and get some white ones on."

At first I wasn't all that happy with being a radioman, mainly because I thought my abilities were being wasted. I was a lot more mechanically inclined than typing tests and listening to Morse code. I had worked on cars since I was ten and had my first car at fourteen. I had completely rebuilt engines by myself. I figured I could handle a bigger and better machine than a typewriter.

After I'd put in a couple of years, I planned to get out and go home to Charleston and resume my pipefitting work. Then one day they sent me to take the third class test and take the day off, so I rushed through it. When the results came back, three out of twelve had passed, and I was one of them.

Then when I came home to Charleston, I saw there were no jobs. There was a long line of people outside of the union hall who were wanting to sign up for the Pipefitters Union, so I got in line. As I got closer and closer, I decided to stay in the Navy to have a job.

At the time they had this program called STAR, which stood for Selective Training and Retention. What that meant was that if you were in a critical rate—which I was—they'd guarantee you a good school, and you could re-enlist for six years and get a bonus of a month's pay for every year you reenlisted.

I reenlisted and got into B school. Only chiefs and first class were allowed to go to B school, but the STAR program allowed second and third class a chance to go. It was a year-long school in how to repair electronic equipment.

I had always done fairly well in school and I enjoyed learning something new, plus repairing equipment seemed just right for me, so I thought this was a good turn of events. What could go wrong? Well, I was about to find out.

I did well in there. A little too well, actually. See, I was young and hadn't been out of high school that long, and

I was in a class with mainly first class and chiefs who'd been in the Navy—and therefore out of the classroom—for a while.

The first four weeks were math. On the first test, I finished first, way ahead of everyone else. The instructor asked if I wanted to review it, but I told him I didn't need to.

When I went back after lunch, he passed out the tests. All except mine. After the class he called me into the next room and accused me of cheating. I told him I didn't cheat, but he said I must have, because no one could get all the answers right. I told him it wasn't that hard, and that just made him mad.

I aced the next tests too, and each time he tried to figure out how I was cheating.

Finally, he decided to make up the test the night before and keep it with him the whole time so no one could get their hands on the answers. I passed that one too.

After that he believed that I actually knew the material well enough to pass.

Dad eventually became good friends with the instructor and his wife (because of course he did). And he graduated in the top five percent of the class, which automatically advanced him to second class.

Making first class was a totally different experience. Rather than coursework that led to promotion, it was a task while he waited for orders.

At that time, Vietnam was a full-blown conflagration, and Dad, having a family that included three small children, wanted to stay stateside.

He requested orders for any ship on the East Coast, preferably Charleston, Norfolk, or Jacksonville. While he waited for word, the detailer encouraged him to take the test, which he did—and did it in a hurry and with-

out having studied. Guess what happened?

Five of us took the test. Three of the men were single, and they had all put in for orders to Vietnam. I wanted anything but Vietnam. Turns out I was the only one who received orders to Vietnam. I tried to swap with one of them, but the request was denied. When I asked the detailer why, he said the billet was for a first class, and I was the only one who had passed the test. That's how I found out I'd made first class.

Dad passed the chief's test easily, but "making chief" wasn't without incident. There are certain rituals and initiations one must endure first.

It's said that one of the main requirements for making chief is being able to walk across the ship with a full cup of coffee without spilling it. With the years I'd spent at sea, I knew I could do that.

Making chief involved some general harassment and hazing. Most of the time it was more or less harmless, but sometimes it could get aggravating. I was one of the few who managed to avoid it.

I had arrived in Lakehurst, New Jersey, as a first class. In the communications center, we worked on machines that used purple fluid. Because of that, they allowed me to wear khakis, which was the working uniform for chiefs.

So, for about two months before I made chief, I was already wearing a chief's uniform. Which meant most people thought I was already chief, so I wasn't targeted for any hazing.

Up there, they had a billet for one chief radioman. They had three already, and when I made chief I'd be the fourth. As time got closer to making chief, they were deciding what my job would be.

Since they had one job between three of them, I volunteered to be a watch stander. They all agreed and appreciated my volunteering. They didn't want to do anything that would keep me from standing watch, so they didn't harass me.

So what was it like to be a chief? One incident seemed to sum it up.

When we lived in Cape Hatteras, I went to Fort Bragg to take a class in taxes so I could do taxes for everyone on base. That way people wouldn't have to go to Nags Head or Norfolk to have their taxes done.

Now, Fort Bragg is an Army/Air Force base, and they didn't have proper quarters for a Navy chief. I told them it was okay, that I could bunk with the other E-7s, but they wouldn't allow that. They said I could be placed in a higher rank, but not a lower one. They ended up placing me with the officers.

But they apologized for the insult.

If you can't pay attention, take notes...

... when the unit you're in is the first to arrive on shore even before the Marines and the Seals

The Navy is known as the country's "first line of defense," which is especially true of the Beachmasters.

After the six-month school in Bainbridge, Maryland, Dad was assigned to Beachmaster Unit Two in Little Creek, Virginia.

Beachmaster Unit Two has been around since 1942, they've provided tactical support in every war or major conflict, and their motto is "This Beach Is Mine."

Dad could've added "And So Is The Drive To The Beach." Here's his tale:

I don't know if this is still the case, but back then the casualty rate for the Beachmaster Unit was 80 or 90 percent, because they were the first on the beach.

Before the Marines, even before the Seals, the Beachmasters went in. They had to set up communications so the Marines and Seals would know where to go.

With the Beachmasters, all of the radio equipment was installed in jeeps, and we made the beach landings so we could have communications on the beach, then we directed the small boats that were carrying the Marines onto the beach.

I was with the Beachmaster unit a couple of years and went with them to the Mediterranean to do exercises in France, Italy, Turkey, and Greece. We worked with the NATO groups too.

When I came back from the Med, I was still with the Beachmaster Unit, and it was pretty good duty.

I learned how to do surf reports, which entailed looking at the water and sending reports to ships to let them know the wave and wind conditions, and that way they could judge whether to do the beachmaster exercises.

Eventually I was assigned to take a jeep, go down to Fort Story, Virginia (a few miles from Little Creek), and send the reports.

These reports had to be done at 4:00 in the morning.

I spent so much time doing those surf reports that I got pretty good at judging how high the seas were just by noticing the direction and strength of the winds.

Which I could do from my front yard.

After a while, I'd radio the ship in the harbor and send my report while

I was driving down there. I was pretty accurate too.

The reports went to an operations officer on the ship. Sometimes they would radio back and request a second report. By that time, I'd be there and could see the surf for myself. Sure enough, the waves would be exactly as I'd described them earlier. It was amazing how accurate I could be about the ocean from a house several miles away from the beach.

If I reported adverse conditions, the ops officer would radio me and request permission to cancel operations. And I always granted permission.

It was the least I could do for an officer and crew who had no idea what the shore looked like from a few miles out at sea.

If you can't pay attention, take notes...

... when you get reminded that they didn't issue you a family with your seabag

There's an old saying that the Navy doesn't issue you a family with your sea bag.

It's a joke, but it highlights a bitter truth: The military often tends to brush aside any other concerns the person might have to ensure that the military's needs take precedence. At least it did back then.

(Times have changed a bit, and the military has much more consideration for families these days.) Back

in the day, though, that's what went down a time or two.

Take, for instance, when my grandfather died. Dad was on the U.S.S. Everglades in the Mediterranean. Dad's brother Robbie had a hard time getting word to Dad. Finally, he remembered that my grandfather had been good friends with Congressman L. Mendel Rivers. At that time, Rivers was an important member of Congress and head of the House Armed Services Committee. Uncle Robbie called him.

I'll let Dad tell the rest of the story…

As radioman, I was the one who received all the messages on the ship. When word came in, I took the message to the captain.

He read it. Then he looked up at me. Then he read it again.

"This is your father," he said.

"Yes, sir."

He looked at the message again.

"The death notice came from one of the congressman?" he asked.

"Yes, sir."

He looked at it more closely.

"Congressman Mendel Rivers? Head of the Armed Services Committee?"

"Yes, sir."

"I want you on the next plane."

"Aye aye, captain."

That sounded fine, but I ran into trouble right away.

We were in Malta at the time. It's a tiny little island where ships would pull into and we'd repair them.

A plane came in once a day to deliver mail. I caught that flight out and went to Naples to try to catch a flight there.

Normally they'd go to Rota, but the

plane wasn't going there. I could go to Greece, but in Greece the only flight I could get was going back to Naples. Then the only flight out of Naples was going to Malta. After two days I was back where I started.

Finally, I got to Rota and signed in for a flight back to the states. Being on emergency leave, I figured I wouldn't have a hard time.

Then I found out that the flight from Rota to the states was a cargo flight coming from Maguire Air Force Base in New Jersey and had ten seats, which were all taken.

The clerk who signed me in for standby noticed that I was a radioman and asked if I had my records with me and whether I had clearance. He said if I had clearance, he can get me on the first flight out of here.

They bumped someone from the flight and I wound up as a courier to get to my father's funeral.

When I finally got to Charleston, my leave was for fifteen days. I tried to extend my leave because Pat was pregnant and due any day, but they said no. I had to return to the ship.

On the day I left Charleston, I flew to Maguire Air Force Base. I was in Maguire when the baby was born, but I didn't get the message until I got back to the ship.

As soon as I got back, they raised the gangplank and we got underway and headed back to the states.

When Dad got back from the Med, he was stationed in Lakehurst, New Jersey. He requested leave so he could be home for Christmas, but they denied the request.

So we did what a lot of military families do in such situations. We celebrated Christmas early.

Dad told us kids (we were ages 11, 7, 4, and newborn) that he had made a call to Santa and was able to get our presents delivered early because Santa is very patriotic and works with military families to get things done early.

We believed him completely. ☕

If you can't pay attention, take notes...

... when most of your job requires staying on the good side of your detailer

This is what it says on the official website for Navy Personnel Command:

Enlisted Detailers are charged with the equitable distribution of Sailors to commands based on billets authorized (BA) and the Navy Manning Plan (NMP) via the Career Management System Interactive Detailing (CMS-ID).

Primary consideration for selection for orders should consid-

er each of the following:

Needs of the Navy, career needs of the individual, and desires of the individual.

And this is what everyone in the Navy has to say about that:

"Hahahahahahaha!"

Being in the Navy means getting sent hither and yon at the whim of the detailer, and heaven help you if you ever cross him.

Getting the duty you want is like an urban myth, and most people in the military have the stories to prove it. Here are a few of Dad's.

One of my first sea duties was a minesweeper out of Charleston, the USS *Rival* (MSO-468). At that point it was at GITMO down in the Caribbean, so I got on a ship that was headed that way.

It was slow going because we were escorting a tiny little ship, the USS

Nahant (AN-83). I remember looking way down over the side and watching it bounce around on the ocean and saying I hoped I never got on a ship that small.

The *Rival* was small too, but it wasn't as tiny as the *Nahant*. Besides, I ended up spending hardly any time on it. A few months after I was stationed on the *Rival*, I developed a cyst on my spine, which required surgery. Afterward I had to stay attached to the hospital for several months until it completely healed.

After a week I was allowed to go home in the evenings, but I had to go back every day to do duty. They assigned me to the Red Cross to show movies in the different wards. Usually they hired a civilian for that task, but since the Navy loaned me to them, they paid me extra.

After my spine healed, I had to go back to all the receiving stations to check back in, and when I got to dental, the captain (the dentist) said I needed some work done, so he put me on dental hold for six months.

All this time—still technically attached to the *Rival*—I was drawing proficiency pay for being in a critical rate.

When the dental work was done, I went back to the receiving stations and found out that I might have to pay back the proficiency pay. The detailer said the only way to avoid that was to get stationed back on the *Rival*—and he said that was probably not going to happen. The detailer can be a real killjoy sometimes.

Well, a lot he knew, because my orders came back from Washington that I was back on the *Rival*. The problem was the *Rival* wasn't in Charleston. It was in the Med and wouldn't be back for a couple of weeks. They weren't going to fly me over to the Med, and I couldn't just stay in Charleston doing nothing until they got back.

We were at a stalemate. Luckily a chief was in there and heard the whole thing. He said he might be able to help. An admiral was going on a two-week cruise to Florida on a minesweeper repair ship and needed a radioman. I could do that and stay attached to the *Rival*.

That wasn't bad duty at all. I would gather his messages every morning and have coffee with him while he read them. The rest of the time I just stayed out of the way, usually napping.

When we got to Key West and were having our morning coffee, he asked me if I had any plans for the rest of the day. I was at his disposal the whole time, so I told him I had no plans, wondering what was up.

Turns out he just wanted to go deep sea fishing and took me with him.

The next day there was a mess and berthing inspection. As usual, I was staying out the way—in the bunk taking a nap. The Master at Arms came through the room and saw me.

"Who the hell do you think you are?" he yelled.

"I'm the admiral's radioman," I said.

His expression changed. "Oh. Carry on."

On the way back to Charleston, the admiral had them stop the ship and put his barge over the side. Then he and I, plus the crew that operated the barge, went fishing while the ship circled around us for a few hours. I wondered what the detailer would think about that.

When we got back my orders had come in. I was being transferred from the *Rival* to another ship, and I was to report to Detyens Shipyard.

I went over there and they took me to my new ship. It was over the side and down a gangplank. I looked down and saw it was the ship I hoped I'd never get on: none other than the USS *Nahant*.

When I got on board, I met the guy I was relieving. Then I met another guy who said I was his relief. I figured I was now doing two jobs. The detailer might be getting his revenge.

I was on the *Nahant* for about a year. Not long after I'd been stationed on it, I had volunteered to go into the submarines. It was better pay, and I thought it probably couldn't be too much worse than this. But then something happened to change my opinion of sub duty.

We took the ship up to Newport, Rhode Island, to clean a training net. I don't know if it could rightly be called a ship; it was a boat: 110 feet, built on a tug's hull. And it was slow. The captain told me to call into Newport and request to enter port and get a berthing assignment. They came back and asked how many tugs we required. We laughed at that. No tugs necessary; we just needed to meet the pilot.

As we readied to go back to Charleston, we got a message that all ships within so many miles of Boston should report to the last known coordinates of a submarine that had just been overhauled and was out on sea trials. It was the USS *Thresher* (SSN-593), lost with all hands—129 crew and shipyard personnel.

At that point I withdrew my request to go into the subs—before the detailer was able to transfer me to a sub.

On the *Nahant* I was the only radioman. I had one assistant—an ET (electronics technician) who had to stand watches with me because I couldn't be in there twenty-four hours. I taught him to recognize our call sign, plus two other pieces of code: AS (which meant "wait") and AR (which meant "out"). That's the only way I could get any sleep.

The *Nahant* had only the captain, an

XO, and an ops officer, so I had underway LDO (limited duty officer) responsibilities. Headed back to Charleston, we were using LORAN for navigation, and I was doing plotting and looking for the "Two Charlie" sea buoy that sits at the entrance to Charleston Harbor.

We were supposed to stay within nine knots, but I took it up to ten knots because I wanted to get home early. Trouble was, that made the ship rattle. The captain came flying onto the bridge asking what the hell was going on. I told him I wanted to get to Charleston earlier.

"You get it back down to nine knots," he said. "We'll get there when we get there."

What could I say? "Aye aye, captain!"

When I left the *Nahant*, I went on shore duty for two years in Pensacola, Florida. On the day I arrived, I went to disbursing to get paid. The date was

November 23, 1963. I ended up getting overpaid because the person behind the desk was talking nonstop about the president being shot and wasn't paying attention to my pay.

I was in Pensacola for two years at Helicopter Training Squadron Eight. The sign over the top of the gate read: "The Best Navy Helicopter Pilots Are Trained Here." Which I thought was strange because it was the *only* helicopter training squadron for the Navy. You better hope they were the best.

After Pensacola I moved my family back to Charleston and tried to get on a ship out of Charleston, or somewhere close. While I waited, I took the test for first class. When orders came, I was the only one who received orders to Vietnam—even though three others had put in for it. I tried to swap with one of them, but I couldn't. I asked the detailer why and he said the billet was for a first class and I was the only one who passed the test.

After Vietnam I finally did get a ship out of Charleston, which I stayed on for almost three years. The USS *Everglades* (DD-24) was a destroyer tender, and the captain was known as "Captain Can-Do." No matter what the situation was, he made sure we figured out how to resolve it, and you didn't turn a job down.

One time I was helping another ship repair their teletype machine. They had six of them to repair, which they sent over to us in boxes. We needed to finish fixing them before the ship got underway. The captain told me if I finished them before the ship got to the sea buoy, I could ride the pilot boat back; if not, I'd have to go with them to Rota, Spain. I came back on the pilot boat.

When my tour was up, we were on a Med cruise, and I had to stay on the ship because they didn't have the funds to fly my relief to the Med. Just before we came back from the Med,

I was called back to Charleston on emergency leave when my father died. They flew me home and back to the ship, but they couldn't send the guy relieving me.

When we got back I was transferred to Lakehurst. The detailer said that was the only available shore duty. I requested additional leave to stay in Charleston for Christmas, but my request was denied.

After I'd been there in New Jersey a while, I kept putting in requests to transfer, even agreeing to terminate shore duty to go back on sea duty if I could get a ship out of Charleston.

I made an appointment to go down to Washington and talk to the detailer. When I finally got in to see him, I had a list of all the ships in Charleston that rated chief radiomen and didn't have one. I had contacted all of them and knew the story. And here, he said he had already taken care of it—although he never did say what he had done.

(I was suspicious that he hadn't done anything and was just saying whatever came to mind to get me out of his office.)

After a few minutes he got up and said he had to take his wife to get groceries. I was upset that I'd set up this appointment to meet with him and he couldn't even give me a half hour. So I wrote a letter to his superior telling him what I thought of detailers in general and this one in particular.

Not long after that, I received orders to report in one week to a helicopter carrier in Norfolk. The next day the ship got underway for the Med. I spent my time in the Med being flown in helicopters to other ships to repair their teletype machines.

In my final encounter with the detailer, he sent me to isolated duty at the Naval Facility in Cape Hatteras. Most people hate that kind of duty because there's usually nothing to do. In this case, the detailer probably thought he was getting back at me for the letter I wrote, but he actually did me a favor.

He had no idea he'd just sent me to the best fishing spot on the East Coast.

I'd finally won against him.

Checkmate.

If you can't pay attention, take notes...

... when training for war includes knowing how to play poker and pinochle

Dad went to Vietnam in November of 1965, right in the thick of it.

I know what it was like from our perspective. I was young at the time, but I remember Mom crying when he had to leave and then later mailing him care packages and taking our photos to send to him.

I'm sure it was hard over there— I've read enough about how bad things were—but he chose to remember the funny moments. Beginning

with survival school...

Survival school was an eight-week course in San Diego that included a couple of weeks in the Mojave Desert.

Why I had to learn to survive in the desert when I was going to a jungle terrain is beyond me, but we had to do it. Knowing how to live on bugs and snakes must have been an important life skill for war.

I'd never heard anything good about the survival school. Most of the time people just got through it as best as they could and sometimes came out of it sick or injured or worse. I figured those two months would amount to the longest year of my life.

When I got there, I found out it was shortened to two weeks. I counted myself lucky until I heard the reason why: They were building up troops and didn't have time to send us through the school.

Not having time to learn to survive

didn't sound too good.

I met some of the fellows who'd spent those weeks out in the desert. By the looks of them—all skinny and sickly looking—I'm thinking they had to shorten our survival school because they'd already eaten the bugs and snakes, and there weren't any left.

When it was time to go, they loaded us up on a C-130 headed to Hawaii for a quick stop before Vietnam.

Now, ordinarily the C-130 was a very reliable heavy-duty cargo plane. But in our case, something kept breaking down on it—the fuel line, then the propeller, then the windshield—and we kept having to return to San Diego.

It took us three tries to get to Hawaii. Every time we had a delay, several of us passed the time playing poker. By the time we finally did get to Hawaii, I'd won several hundred dollars. I was starting to think that war duty wasn't so bad after all.

When Dad got to Vietnam, there were other sources for amusement. Like the marine who lost the pin in his hand grenade...

Our base controlled the entire harbor of Da Nang, and we monitored communications with the ships.

One night I was standing watch when I got a call from a marine on one of the ships. He had gotten bored standing watch, so he was playing with his grenade, tossing it from one hand to the other, and the pin fell out. He held on to it tight and managed to make a call to ask me what to do.

"Let me get this straight," I said. "You're standing there with a live grenade in your hand, and you want to know what to do about it?"

"Yes, sir!" he said.

I gave him the best advice I had. "Don't fall asleep."

After he got a good chuckle out of it, Dad told him to throw it as far as he could into the water, and he let the other ships know that the explosion wasn't enemy fire.

As for his card-playing, in the year he was stationed there, he managed to win more than $3,000—a nice tidy sum back in those days that allowed him to buy a piece of land when he came home.

While I was there I played poker a lot, but I also got really good at pinochle. In fact, most of the money I won was from playing pinochle—although it was all in MPCs (military pay chits).

That didn't matter, though, because I kept track of the stacks of chits. I'd cash them in one by one later to avoid any suspicion that I'd been gambling.

But then one night, I had just come off of midwatch and had just fallen asleep when the chief came in and woke me up and asked if I was ready to go.

I had worked for this chief for a

while and had attended a lot of meetings with him, so I figured we were off to a meeting. I asked where we were going.

"If you can be at the airport at 2:00 in the afternoon, you can go home," he said.

I told him don't worry, I'd be ready. It took me all of five minutes to pack.

Except I had all those chits to cash in. There wasn't time to cash them on various paydays. I had to go to disbursing and fill out a form. They said they couldn't cash them without the XO's approval.

I was a little worried. Gambling was frowned upon, and I couldn't figure out how to explain how I came upon this much money in MPCs.

I decided to just tell the truth and see what happened.

I went to the XO and told him I'd won the money playing cards and wanted to cash it in before I headed back to the states.

He stared at me for a minute, and I thought he was going to chew me out.

"You won this much money playing poker?" he asked.

"No, sir. Pinochle."

He looked through all the chits again. His eyebrows shot up and he shrugged his shoulders.

"Not bad," he said.

He signed my request, and I headed home.

If you can't pay attention, take notes...

... when Robert Mitchum stops by for a few beers

In 1941 the United Service Organizations (USO) partnered with the Department of Defense to help provide services for the armed forces. Although not part of the government, the organization has a congressional charter and relies on private funding of money and goods.

In World War II, the USO began a tradition of entertaining the troops overseas—in particular, the live performances called "Camp Shows" to boost the morale of the troops. The shows have continued through all of the wars our country has been through, including the Vietnam War.

Vietnam is where Dad met a few of his Hollywood idols...

The USO show was a big treat. There wasn't much entertainment on base—unless you played cards—and everyone wanted to see the show when it came by. They tried to arrange it so everyone who wanted to go could go. Bob Hope and Ann-Margret came to Da Nang, and we saw them on stage.

Ann-Margret was beautiful. She really made the show. And she looked so glad to be there, so glad to be entertaining all of us. I read later how much it meant to her to come there and how she always thought of us as "her gentlemen." To this day, everyone who was there feels special to be one of her gentlemen.

And everyone loved Bob Hope. I know he did a lot of movies and TV shows, but I think his best performance was the USO show. I think it was because he was so determined to make us laugh—and in the middle of a war zone—that he was so authentic.

Everyone on the base felt so good afterward. I don't know if the people who traveled with the USO ever knew how much that meant to us.

Another thing that meant a lot was when some of the performers would come to the barracks to see us personally. John Wayne came one time to talk to us, joking around about how he wasn't sure he could be in a war if he didn't have a horse to ride and how nothing he ever did would measure up to what we were doing. He was a real stand-up guy.

But I tell you, the best time we had was when Robert Mitchum visited our barracks. He had a few beers with us and started telling stories. His assistants kept telling him he had to move on but he waved them off and kept talking to us.

We had the best time talking to him. His assistants would lean in and remind him that the officers were waiting for him, but he yelled back that he wasn't interested in seeing them because they wouldn't give him any beer.

Of course, that was our cue to hand him another beer, which we did, and he kept going.

He finally left and went off to the officers' quarters—about two hours late—but we all felt like we'd made a life-long friend.

A lot of people think that Robert Mitchum's greatest contribution to the world was his acting ability in the roles he played. Don't get me wrong, I think he was a great actor.

But I can tell you that one of the things that made him a really honorable man was when he made a group of first-class petty officers feel like spending time with them was all he wanted to do.

If you can't pay attention, take notes...

... when you spend an hour dressing up to meet the ship at Pier Papa

I studied my reflection in the mirror. I had on my prettiest dress and my new shoes. Would he still think I was as pretty as ever? I heard the horn honking outside, so stopped wondering and dashed out to the car.

The big day was finally here. The man I loved most in the whole world was coming back and I couldn't wait to see him.

All the way to the Naval base I thought of the letters he and I had ex-

changed. I loved reading them. The descriptions of faraway lands never failed to capture my imagination.

Sometimes he sent foreign money, which I loved to carry around and show off. The letters I sent to him carefully spelled out how much I missed him.

At the base we parked in the lot near Pier Papa, the berthing place for the USS Everglades, and strolled down the pier to stand among the other families. We all chatted with each other with the same breathless anticipation.

A murmur of excitement made its way through the crowd. The ship was gliding around the final bend in the channel, headed for the pier. Of all the thrilling sights in the world, a Navy ship returning from a cruise is the one sight guaranteed to leave me exhilarated and tearful at the same time.

The sleek, gray warship moved at

a snail's pace up the Cooper River, inching its way home.

I thought of the long months I'd waited for this very moment and wished they would speed things up.

They sailors were lined up on the quarterdeck, and I tried to catch a glimpse of him. Unfortunately, all sailors look alike in uniform. I worried that when he came off the ship I would miss him.

The tugboats pushed the ship the last couple of yards. My self-control was beginning to give way. I started tapping my foot. An eternity later the mooring lines were secured and the brow was brought to the quarterdeck. I looked up at the enormous gray giant and saw the "D 24" painted on the side. The numbers were bigger than I was.

Finally, they started streaming off the ship. There were reunions everywhere but not yet for us. I searched ev-

ery face, hoping the next smile would be for me. Where was he? I looked behind me, wondering if he had walked by without my noticing.

I turned back—and there he was: the dark hair and dark eyes I had known since I was born, the eyes shining in a smile.

He waved and called my name, and I heard the voice that had calmed and cheered me all my life. I watched that same clipped, determined walk that I remembered and knew nothing would keep him from reaching me. I broke away and raced to him.

As he scooped me up, I squealed in delight, as eager as any five-year-old when she sees her daddy again for the first time in six very long months.

If you can't pay attention, take notes...

... when you commandeer a jeep from the Army and it's too much paperwork for them to claim it

My dad always had a way with vehicles. A magic touch, you might say. And it wasn't just making it run smoothly; his ability to get vehicles for little or nothing was an art.

Take the time he found a jeep in perfect condition. Not bought, not borrowed: found. And he got to keep it courtesy of the U.S. Army. It might have been his best auto purchase, considering there was no purchase. But I'll let him tell the story his way.

I had been transferred from the main communications centers to the harbor entrance control post. That post controlled all the shipping and boats, including fishing boats, in and out of the harbor of Da Nang.

Transportation from our barracks to the post was "iffy" most of the time. The buses were usually broken down or if they worked, then they couldn't find a driver. We ended up walking the three miles almost every day.

After I'd been there about three months, I found a jeep.

I was walking to work with Bill, a guy who worked in Operations. Same building where I worked, down the hall from my office. We stood watch together a lot, so we usually made the trip to the post together.

This one day, we were walking along, and as we rounded a corner, we saw an Army jeep on the side of the road.

We thought it was odd. Here's this jeep out in the middle of nowhere, just sitting there. Bill and I walked around it and looked it over good just in case it was booby-trapped. We didn't find anything, so we got in and hit the starter. What luck—it cranked right up!

We didn't know why anyone had abandoned the jeep, but we were going to take advantage of the free ride.

Then we went about two feet and realized why it was just sitting there abandoned. The tie rod had come loose, and the front wheels were headed in different directions.

Good thing we had left the barracks early that morning—since it looked like the bus wasn't going to make it again—because we had time to run back and get some bailing wire to tie up the rods. We did, and we fixed it up.

But then Bill and I got to thinking. The Army might be coming back for it, possibly with their motor pool—

or worse, with armed guards—and it wouldn't do for us to have it in our possession. So instead of driving off with it, we left it there.

When we got off work the next morning, we saw it was still there. Now most of us in the Navy didn't have a terribly high opinion of the Army, but we knew that even they wouldn't take twenty-four hours to fix a jeep. So we drove it back to the barracks. We figured they'd come looking for it, and we'd let them know we fixed it.

They never did, though. We drove it back and forth for several days until it finally ran low on fuel.

We took it over to the Navy fuel depot. A supply clerk filled it up and noticed that it was an Army jeep, not one of ours.

I started to pay for it, but the fellow said he'd charge it to the Army.

"No, that's all right," I told him. "I'll pay for it."

"Nope. It's the Army's jeep. They'll pay."

What the heck, I let 'em pay. Who am I to argue with military protocol?

So we kept driving it. Then about a month later, Bill took it into town. He stopped in at the club, had a few drinks, and ended up staying out past curfew. The MPs arrested him, and he called me for help.

By this time, he was in deeper trouble than just staying out past curfew. He was a sailor driving an Army jeep with no papers, and no one believed his story about finding it on the side of the road and fixing it.

I caught a ride over there after my watch was over, and I explained everything to the provost marshal.

At first the provost marshal didn't believe me either, especially when he found out I was a radioman. Not that a radioman can't work on cars, but this man just wasn't buying the story.

I told him all about my background working on cars and all, and he finally took my word for it. But he was still fit to be tied.

Turns out the jeep had already been marked as transferred stateside and taken out of their inventory. It would create a lot of paperwork and probably start an investigation if they acknowledged that it was still in Vietnam.

He sat there, his face getting redder and redder, and he glared at both of us. Finally, he passed sentence.

"Just keep it!" he said. "But don't tell anyone around here where you got it."

We agreed. He closed the case. Then he had his motor pool fix the front end for us.

And we had free gas for the rest of our tour.

All we had to do was pull up to the depot and tell them to fill it up and charge it to the Army.

If you can't pay attention, take notes...

... when you're mistaken for NIS simply because you commute to the ship via helicopter

After Dad made chief in New Jersey, he was stationed on the USS Guam (LPH-9), a helicopter carrier.

Even though it was based in Norfolk, every Monday it went down off the coast of South Carolina to test the new vertical-lift helicopter (now known as the Harrier) that were being developed in Beaufort.

And that's where he was involved in a rather amusing case of mistaken identity.

It just so happened that Pete was stationed on the ship the same day I was. He and I had a lot in common. Not only were we both in communications and both chiefs, but we also were both from South Carolina (he was from Florence).

We also had the same NEC (Navy Enlisted Classification) code for classified equipment, and that got us into different places on the ship that not everyone had access to.

Because we were repairing teletype machines, it was better for us to work in the middle of the night (when incoming messages were less frequent), and the captain let us do as we pleased as long as we kept the machines running.

Most of the time we worked about three hours a night, and otherwise just wandered around not doing any other work. There were other chiefs on board, so we rarely went into the radio room.

All of that—odd hours, having free reign, the captain leaving us alone—led some people to believe we with Naval Intelligence.

At first, we didn't notice. But before long we had a hard time finding people to play pinochle with. And then people started giving us worried looks when we tried to strike up conversations.

Well, by then we knew something was up. Finally, one of the men in communications told us why some people were wary of us.

And then our reputation was sealed when Pete and I requested—and received approval—from the captain to take the mail helicopter out on Fridays to Charleston and come back on Monday mornings.

Who else could do that except somebody working undercover?

Pete and I figured it wasn't all bad. Being mistaken for NIS did keep the aggravation to a minimum. The office on watch never bothered us. No one nagged us for reports. We could do pretty much anything we wanted.

Except make any money on cards. For some reason we couldn't find anyone who would admit to playing the game. ☕

If you can't pay attention, take notes...

... when you have to dun the mob for $375

You know, sometimes you're just trying to provide a little more for your family and you take on extra work and somehow you end up working for the mob—or what appears to be mob-like. It happens.

But then, the mob wasn't such an easy thing to discern back then. There was no "Sopranos" or "Law & Order" we could turn to for comparison.

Suffice it to say that when push came to shove—as it did when they didn't pay him for the work he did—

Dad stood his ground. One could interpret that as "not being compromised."

One could also interpret that as "what, are you nuts, they're the mob!"

Whatever the case, here's what happened, as Dad tells it.

When we were in Lakehurst, I did some plumbing and construction side work for a company when I wasn't on duty at the base.

Initially I didn't suspect anything underhanded was going on. I worked, I got paid. It was good work, and I was glad to have the extra money.

Then after a few months they asked me to help out with one of their other enterprises, a security guard company.

So I became a night watchman too, guarding some properties they had contracted with.

Turns out the security guard company was a busy place. They were guarding a lot of companies within a five-mile area, and I ended up with a crew working under me, mostly guys I recruited from the base.

I ran a tight schedule around their off-duty liberty time.

Most of the time it was quiet—a little boring, in fact. Just sitting and watching a building for a couple of hours.

But now and then something would happen that would make your heart start pumping.

Like the night I was watching a construction company. I checked on it, saw that all was fine, and drove off to see about a few other places.

I came back thirty minutes later and saw the gates were open. I got out with my flashlight, went in there, and found two men working on a piece of equipment.

I shined my light on them.

"Hey, what do you think you're doing?" I was nervous but disguised it with a sharp voice.

One of the men flashed his light back at me.

"What do you think *you're* doing?"

"I want to know what you're doing," I said again.

"What the hell is that to you?"

"I'm security," I said.

"You got any proof of that?" he asked.

The whole time we've both got our lights in each other's eyes. It occurred to me that if we were holding guns, things would be going downhill right about now.

I noticed the other guy standing next to him. I was outnumbered. Good thing we *didn't* have guns.

"Do you have some ID?" I asked.

"Do you have any ID?" he asked

right back.

It was like talking to a parrot.

Finally I told him my name and the name of the company I was working for. Not to be outdone, he told me he was the owner of the building I was guarding.

Being at an impasse, we had no choice but to shut off our flashlights with assurances we'd follow up the next day to find out if each other was telling the truth.

The next day I found out two things: 1) He actually *was* the owner, and 2) I left such an impression that he requested I be the only one guarding his place.

I guess it helps to know how to wield a flashlight.

Our guard duty involved more than watching buildings. We guarded two egg packing plants, and we'd have to escort the trucks.

Believe it or not, at that time one of the items stolen most often in New Jersey was eggs. Apparently they're something that can't be traced, especially after broken.

At any rate, they had a big problem with people hijacking the trucks and stealing the eggs.

Both my mother and my grandmother used to keep chickens, and up to this point, I never knew eggs were such a valuable commodity. Had I known, I might have taken more care when my chores involved going into the coops.

Guarding those packing plants was not my favorite thing, mainly because the trucks would leave at 3:00 or 4:00 in the morning, and we'd escort them to the last stop light out of town. Beyond that they were on their own.

I started to get an inkling that things might be a little dodgy when I was watching a building and the owner decided he didn't need security anymore. There was no animosity or anything. It was just that we'd been watching their building for a long time and nothing had happened, so he figured he could save the expense of a security system.

My boss came to me and told me to take the next night off. When I said I could work anyway, he said he'd pay me, but he wanted me to stay home. Well, the next night, what do you know, that company was ransacked and, amazingly, they decided they did need security after all.

The full state of the company's principles (or lack of) came to light a few months later. I was standing watch and got a call saying a few New Jersey state policemen were at the gate and wanted to talk to me. I couldn't let them in the building—we were in a security facility—so I met them after work.

It was just like a scene in a movie. They pushed me into the back of their car and started asking me questions about the company I'd been working for. I told them I didn't know anything, but they started telling me dates and times and places I worked. They already had all the information.

"We're not after you," they assured me. "We're after the people you're working for."

They opened their notepads and started in with all they knew.

They knew how much I got paid and the other guys who were working for me. They knew their names, where they worked on the base, whether they were single or had families, and exactly how much they had made on the side work.

"They'll go down too if you don't cooperate," they said.

I didn't know what to say. All I could do was sit there thinking just how deep I was in it. They saw the look on my face.

"We know you're in the military," one of them said, "and we appreciate the job you're doing."

Well there was that. Never let it be said the state police in New Jersey aren't patriotic.

"You can help us or you can hinder us," the other one said. "If you help us, we don't know you. No one will ever know that we talked to you. And you won't have to appear in court—we'll see to that. If you don't help us, it won't go so well."

These guys certainly knew how to drive a bargain.

I told them I really didn't know anything other than the work I was doing, which they already seemed to have a full record of.

They said they were going to ask me questions and I could just verify whether they were correct.

The questions they asked were mostly about dates, times, and places I worked—which seemed odd, considering they already had all that information. After a while, they let me go. One of them gave me his card and told me to call if I ever needed anything.

Shortly after that, I left New Jersey and was headed to the *Guam* for a Med cruise. The company I'd been working for still owed me $375. I called and reminded them about it, and they said they'd put a check in the mail that day.

The check never came.

I called back. They said they were on their way to Western Union to wire the money.

It never came.

I called every day for a week, and each time they said they were taking care of it right that minute. Of course, they never were.

The time when I had to report to the ship was getting closer. I finally figured I needed help. I pulled out the policeman's business card and gave him a call. After I explained the situation, he said he'd take care of it. I figured I'd hear back in roughly six months, about the time I'd be getting back from the Med cruise.

Someone from their department called me the next morning and said she could verify that I was owed $360, not $375. She could send me a check that day or I could protest and open an investigation. I told her the $360 was just fine. The check arrived two days later.

I never heard anything else about it. I have no idea what happened to the owners of that company, what they were being investigated for, or whether they were indicted. My entire contribution was nothing more than verifying a series of questions they already had the answers to. They never got anything from me that they didn't already know.

Except that the company didn't know how to mail a check.

If you can't pay attention, take notes...

... when SecNav sends a helicopter to deliver a gold-plated fishing rod to you

Dad was one of those rare individuals who doesn't care about someone's station in life, financial standing, or any other so-called status symbols. None of that impressed him.

What did matter to him was a person's character and—more important—what sense of humor the person had.

In the Navy, he never buddied up to the brass, even though he had plenty of opportunities. And yet somehow

the brass always managed to find him.

Take the time when we lived in Cape Hatteras and an admiral came down to the island with his wife...

The admiral and his wife didn't want to go fishing. They just wanted to go walking on the beach. So they parked their car at the temporary officer housing and went for a walk.

When they came back, their car wouldn't start.

They contacted the captain, who said he'd get someone to fix it. The admiral assumed he had sent for someone from the mechanic's shop, but Don Barton, the head mechanic (and one of the best mechanics I've ever known), was in the hospital at that time.

The captain said he wouldn't let any of the other mechanics in the shop touch his car, but he had a chief radioman he'd let look at it. He called me and I came right over. I got to know that admiral pretty well, and later he came down and went fishing with me.

When we lived in Cape Hatteras, Dad and his friend Dave started a fishing business. They used to take out fishing parties, sometimes deep-sea fishing and sometimes surf fishing. Most of the parties were tourists, but word spread up to Norfolk and pretty soon officers from up there were calling them.

One of Dad's regulars was Captain Jackson. He and Dad became good friends, and years later, Captain Jackson performed Dad's retirement ceremony.

We realized how far our reputation had spread when we got a message from Washington that a captain wanted to go out fishing and then a week later the captain of our NavFac called us in his office and said the Secretary of the Navy was on his way down and we needed to take him fishing.

I told him I was already taking a captain out that day, so he looked at Dave.

Dave said he was busy preparing for an operations readiness inspection.

The captain said, "Chief, some days your job is to prepare for a readiness inspection, and some days it's your job to take SecNav out fishing. Today, it's your job to go fishing."

Dave gave him a quick salute. "Aye aye, Captain!"

After that, every time he came down to the island, SecNav asked for Dave.

A few months later, we got a message on the teletype: "SecNav's helicopter will land at 1300 hours."

I sent it over to the captain, but I called him anyway. A surprise visit from SecNav is not something a captain is eager to receive. Especially when it's 12:30 and the helicopter would be there in a half hour. Our landing pad was the ball field, and we had to make sure no one was on it.

When I told the captain, he said, "What was the rest of the message?"

"That was all, Captain," I said.

So he and the XO and the rest of the officers gathered on the ball field and waited. Everyone looked nervous, wondering what kind of reaming out he was in for.

Finally the helicopter arrived, and a man got out and handed a package to the captain.

"Give these to the chiefs," he said. The he got back in the helicopter and they took off.

Everybody stood there staring—the captain, the XO, and all those officers.

When the captain got back to his office, he got a call from SecNav telling him to award the package to Dave and me with all due ceremony.

The next morning at quarters, the captain handed each of us a fishing rod with our names engraved in gold.

And he did it with all the ceremony he could muster. Which, to be honest, we thought was a little lackluster—considering he didn't get the reaming out he had been expecting. ☕

If you can't pay attention, take notes...

... when a fishing buddy turns out to be an undercover agent with NIS

My dad was a friendly guy. He never had a problem striking up a conversation, and he could talk about anything.

And if the conversation veered off into unfamiliar territory, he would just start talking about fishing.

I used to say that he never met a stranger. But that was before I heard the story of his good friend who just happened to assume different roles for the sake of his job.

When I was stationed in Norfolk, I met a fellow who worked in the Beachmaster unit with me.

Mike was a second class boatswain's mate and had been for a long time.

You could tell by the stripes up his arm that he'd been taking the first class test for a while and obviously hadn't passed it yet. The boatswain's mate first class test was hard to pass.

That didn't seem to bother him, though. He was a nice, easy-going guy—loved to tell jokes and play cards and fish. We had a lot in common.

Mike was married and had two kids. We went fishing all the time, and he and his wife came over and played cards with me and Pat. Over the course of a year, we got to know them pretty well. We even went on vacation together.

One day two military police came to the door of our building. Mike was standing between them. The MPs asked to come in to talk to a particular chief who was on duty. I told them it was a secure building and I couldn't let them in, but if they would wait there, I'd go get him.

I found the chief and took him to the door, and the MPs arrested him.

The whole time Mike didn't look at me. I was worried about what kind of trouble he was in.

I found out from some others in the building that the chief they arrested was suspected of selling answers to the first class test. Now I was really worried about Mike.

As soon as I got off duty, I went to his house to see his wife and let her know I was going to the brig to see Mike.

But when I got there, the house was completely empty. All of it was gone—the furniture, their clothes, the food in the refrigerator. Nothing was left. No moving boxes, nothing in sight.

By this time I was thoroughly confused, but I made my way over to the brig and asked if I could see Mike.

He wasn't there. In fact, they had no idea who I was talking about.

When I got home, I told Pat about it. She was shocked. She had just seen Mike's wife in the commissary the day before.

When I got to work the next day, I found out that Mike had been working undercover with Naval Intelligence. They had known for a while that someone was selling secrets to the test, but they weren't sure who it was. Mike—obviously not his real name—had been working on the case all that time.

Several years later I was stationed in Charleston. One day I was walking across the base, when I passed someone who looked familiar. I turned around; he turned around. We stared at each other for a moment.

It was Mike.

But this time he was no longer a second class boatswain's mate. Now he was a chief engineman. He looked surprised, like he didn't know what to say, but then he extended his hand.

"John, how's it going?" he asked.

"It's going good," I said. I wasn't sure what to call him, so I hesitated. "What are you doing here?"

"I'm stationed on the *Sierra*," he said.

I didn't ask him why. I figured he probably couldn't tell me, and whatever he did tell me wouldn't be true.

So we talked about fishing. After about ten minutes, he went on his way and I went on mine.

About a week later, I heard about a drug bust on the USS *Sierra* (AD-18).

I wasn't surprised at all.

I never did see Mike again. At least I don't think I did.

Might depend on how good he was at disguises. ☕

P.S. I always loved this story. I used to wonder what Mike's life was like. How was he able to keep himself from getting found out? Was it a lonely career for him? Was the woman he was with in Norfolk really his wife, or was she another agent? And were those really their children?

I was so intrigued by this character that I put him in a series of novels I wrote (the Para Team 1 series) that involve an agent with a special unit of Naval Intelligence

In my books, his name is Nick Bell. And yes, he does befriend a man named John with whom he goes fishing, and he regrets it deeply when he has to lie to John to maintain the integrity of the case he's working on.

If you can't pay attention, take notes...

... when your career is the least interesting thing about NAVFAC duty

In June of 1972, just coming off a stint on a helicopter carrier and with retirement looming, Dad got the best orders of his Navy career: a tour of duty in Cape Hatteras on the Outer Banks of North Carolina. And what a tour is was...

I received orders to Cape Hatteras when I had about two months left on my enlistment. I had already lined up a job as an electrician at South Carolina Electric & Gas. I figured I'd move up there, see if I liked it, and move the family back after a few months if it didn't work out. If it did work out, I'd extend, but I thought I'd probably be getting out. After two months, I decided to stay.

But those were a crazy two months. To start with, the moving van got lost (from what I understand, the driver got drunk and ditched it), and it took three months for all of our worldly goods to be delivered. Meanwhile, the Navy gave us various pieces to furnish our home in base housing. Which meant when our furniture was delivered, we had double the furniture we needed. But at least we had our clothes when school started.

As we were getting settled in, Dad took care of various issues with the same aplomb he always had...

I had three vehicles at that time, and the base decided to enclose the carport, which meant I couldn't fit any of my vehicles inside. I had to park them in the driveway and on the grass.

There were some complaints about how many cars we had parked on the yard, and it was brought to my attention. Finally, I put in a request to pave the front yard at my own expense. I was called in to explain the situation to the captain. He approved the request. I never did pave it. But I also never heard another complaint again.

Speaking of vehicles, Dad found out about a 1967 Mustang someone wanted to sell because it wouldn't go past second gear. Dad offered $100. The owner was tired of trying to fix it and desperate to get off the island, so they had a deal. But then...

For a couple of weeks, I just kept it in the driveway. Then one day I figured I needed to see what I'd need to do to fix it.

Our neighbor, Don Barton, was the best auto mechanic I knew, and he offered to help me rebuild the transmission. We took it up the road to see what all was wrong with it. We got a few miles, and I thought I heard something. We stopped, and I looked under the car. Turns out the vacuum hose was loose, and that was causing all the trouble. We fixed that, and it worked great ever since.

And speaking yet again of vehicles...

The base had two jeeps that were used for special services, where people could rent them for the day to take out on the beach. Because of weather conditions, lack of upkeep, and general mistreatment, they were in sorry shape and wouldn't run. One of them was good only for pieces and parts; the other wouldn't start.

The mechanics on the base—except for Don, who was in the hospital at the time—tried to get them to run. When they couldn't, the base put them up for auction.

My friend Dave and I decided to put in a bid for them. We heard people saying they'd give $50 for them, so we bid $50.50 for both—and we were the highest bidder.

We had thirty days to get them off the base. The one probably wouldn't ever run, but I was determined to drive the other off the base.

We worked on it all day one Saturday and put a battery in it and drove it off.

Dave and I took about three gallons of bondo and rebuilt the body on it. We drove it for about a year. He drove it for a while, then I drove it for a while, and we let others borrow it.

We had painted it with Navy chromite (a bright yellow primer that was a rust inhibitor), and we planned to repaint it but never did. It looked like a canary going down the road.

One day of the sailors came to us and said he wanted to buy it from us. We told him to make us an offer. He offered $600. Sold!

Soon Dad and Dave met Ken, who asked if they'd like to take a fishing party out. And that's how it all got started.

We started doing fishing parties all the time, taking people surf fishing. I bought a boat and named it *Patricia Ann* (after Mom), and then we started taking out deep sea fishing parties. Sometimes they were tourists, and sometimes they were military people from Washington. Captains and admirals would call the base and ask our captain if there was anyone around who could give them pointers. The captain would hook us up with them.

Dad ended up extending his duty in Cape Hatteras twice. We lived there six years, which for a Navy brat is practically an eternity. Or at least long enough to make it feel like home.

Those six years were filled with crazy antics, enough to fill another book (and maybe that will be the sequel to this book). Even the small mo-

ments could bring a quick chuckle.

Like the time my brother, six years old at the time, asked: "Hey Daddy, after you and Dave, who runs the base?"

That pretty much summed up the state of things on the base.

Busy with two side work businesses—fishing parties and electrical/plumbing work—Dad's Navy career was probably the easiest part of his day.

And yet he was still one of the most respected men on the base. When the officer in communications (his boss) was leaving, he told his replacement to pay attention to everything Chief Hempton said.

After all, chiefs are the ones who run the Navy.

And none did it better than Dad.

If you can't pay attention, take notes...

... when you deserve hazard pay for rescuing Oscar

Training exercises at sea are an interesting time. Occasionally fun. Often tedious. Sometimes dangerous. But always interesting. Especially when it involves an officer making a damn fool of himself.

We were doing exercises out at sea, and the captain was training an ensign. One day he decided to do the Oscar drill, the man-overboard drill where we threw a man-sized styrofoam dummy into the ocean, then declared "man overboard" on the "1-A" loudspeaker system throughout the ship.

At that point, every sailor goes to the muster station to determine who is overboard, while the bridge jumps into action to recover the person who went overboard.

The bridge steers the ship in a "pattern 8"—which means a series of course changes to get back to the original location.

It's designed so they pull up alongside the person in the water.

On this particular training, I was up on bridge and saw what happened.

The ensign was so nervous that when he made the pattern 8 and got back to Oscar, he ran over him. The propeller chewed him up and there was bright orange and white fluff everywhere.

The captain was furious.

He put his hands on his hips, stared down the ensign, and said, "Son, if I ever fall overboard, you just stop the ship and I'll swim to you."

If you can't pay attention, take notes...

... when retirement looks suspiciously like active duty

Just south of Charleston, South Carolina, where tradition has it "the Ashley and Cooper rivers meet to form the Atlantic Ocean," a network of rivers and creeks form the heart of the Lowcountry.

The waterways branch off like arteries and veins and capillaries, the passageways gradually tapered by the pluff mud banks.

That's where you'll find the Bohicket River, which winds its way beyond the fork heading to the Kiawah River, past the site of the annual Rockville Regatta, and eventually into the Great Atlantic. But long before it reaches the ocean, it runs behind Dad's house in a fairly quiet area.

These waters are tidal, and for anglers like Dad and his friend Ken, time is measured in the ebb and flood rather than the clock or calendar. Dad's heart attack six months earlier and Ken's triple bypass a mere three weeks before were incidental. On this day, they both felt fine, the sun was high, and low tide beckoned.

As they cast off in a sixteen-foot boat, they spoke little. In their forty-year friendship, most of those years spent in a boat, conversation was unnecessary. Their common threads—love of the water, service in the Navy, and recent heart surgeries—were understood.

They made their way to the bend in the creek where the trout were almost guaranteed to be running. Dad steered while Ken unfolded his shrimp net, ready to cast for bait. Just as they reached the spot...

We got there and the engine died. I tried pulling the starter a few times and noticed that the throttle was stuck. I flipped it open wide and pulled—and the engine roared, which threw me off balance. I dove into the water, and when I came up, the boat was circling the center of the river, still at full throttle.

After a few moments, I wondered why Ken didn't stop the boat. Just then a head popped up next to me. I looked at him. He looked at me. Then we looked at the boat.

I thought Ken's face looked a little gray and asked him if he was all right. Ken said he wasn't sure he could make it to the bank.

I hooked my arm under Ken's chest and started inching the two of us toward the bank.

This whole time the boat kept circling. When we were a few yards from the bank, I asked Ken if he could float the rest of the way. His breathing was too labored for talk, but Ken nodded.

I started swimming back to the boat. By that time, the engine had sputtered and died. I had to swim against the current, which should have brought the boat closer, but instead the strong winds moved the boat farther away. After a long time, I reached the boat and clung to the side until I could catch my breath.

I finally pulled myself in and made my way to the bank and helped haul Ken on board.

We turned the boat homeward and started paddling—but now we were going against the current.

After an hour of non-stop paddling, we flagged down a passing boater, who towed us the rest of the way. We tied up and sat on the edge of the dock.

We had no fish, no shrimp, and worst of all, Ken lost his wallet to the deeps.

But on the other hand, nothing in the boat fell overboard except the two of us. Our favorite cast nets and fishing rods were still intact. It wasn't a bad day.

They made plans to get a new motor the next morning and install it before low tide. They had to wait until after Dad's doctor appointment, during which he'd be taking a stress test as a follow-up to the surgery when he received two stints. Ken's follow-up doctor appointment was the following week.

Dad said Ken mentioned being sore and that it hurt to breathe.

"That's what happens when you swim against the tide," Dad told him.

"Well, the doctors did tell us to get plenty of exercise," Ken said.

If you can't pay attention, take notes...

... when you have one more story to tell

Dad died on New Year's Day, after a holiday season that was everything he could have wanted. God saw to that, no doubt.

I'm picturing a conversation between Dad and God—presumably in a dream, but who knows, it could have been one day when he was fishing in the river—in which God let him know that his time on Earth was getting short.

I imagine it went something like this:

"No, I don't think I'm ready to go yet," Dad would say. *"I still have some things I need to do."*

"Such as?" God would ask.

"Well, there's my dream house down by the river," Dad would explain. *"I didn't get to build it yet. And I have to be the one to supervise all of it, especially the plumbing and electrical."*

And God would say, "I have a home ready for you here."

And Dad would come back with, "But I have to teach my grandchildren how to throw a cast net."

And I imagine God would be kind and compassionate, but also firm. "No, John. It's time for you to come home with me."

And Dad would fold his arms across his chest, lean back, and look up, thinking of a good way to phrase it so the entire discussion would go his way.

But in the end, he would realize that he was, in fact, trying to win a debate with the Creator of the Universe, and so he eventually would smile and take a deep breath and shrug his shoulders.

"Well, all right, I'll go if you think that's best, but I want to ask you for a couple of things before I go. If that's okay with you."

Dad could be very persuasive, even with the Almighty, but I think God enjoyed him so much that he granted everything Dad wanted.

For instance, Dad loved the holidays—from Halloween through New Year's Day—so much that I think God gave him one last holiday season with his family.

His progressing heart disease became a blessing in disguise as it slowed him down enough to have long heartfelt conversations with everyone around him

At the time it didn't seem like much of a blessing at all, but God knew best: nothing short of heart failure would slow Dad down.

In the week after Christmas, he started to fade fast. I think it was because he had finished everything he wanted to tidy up, including dictating to me his last official letter to family and friends and giving his great-grandson, Bishop, his seven-foot cast net.

The lessons in how to cast it he had to leave to others.

He eased out of this life and into eternity peacefully, with all of his children around him.

But wouldn't you know it—death didn't stop him from getting in one more word. There was the incident with his pacemaker battery.

You see, several months before he died, his pacemaker started beeping, an indication that the battery was running low. There was no danger in it stopping: The pacemaker sent out a warning like this months before it was time to be replaced, so the doctor had time to schedule the procedure.

The doctor had replaced Dad's pacemaker in November, and it worked fine. Unfortunately, the pacemaker only kept the heart rhythm steady; it didn't keep his heart from wearing out, which it finally did.

On the morning he died, the Hospice nurse came to the house, and, as Dad had requested previously (and we had agreed), at the moment of death, she put a special magnet over Dad's heart to prevent the defibrillator from shocking his heart and trying to start it again. Eventually the pacemaker stopped, and he was gone.

A few days later, the family gathered at the funeral home an hour before everyone else came. He had asked to be buried in his work uniform, so we stood over his casket and put spe-

cial items in his shirt pockets—like his notebook and pens, photos of his family, things that were meaningful to him.

As we were doing this, all of a sudden the pacemaker started beeping.

We all had a staring contest.

My sisters and brother were speechless, but I started laughing.

It was just like Dad to have something hilarious happen at his funeral.

My husband ran to get the funeral director, who came in and assured us that nothing like this had ever happened before.

Of course it hadn't. Because something like this would only happen to Dad.

The beeping finally stopped, and we calmed down a bit. A few minutes later people started arriving for the visitation, and I pulled some of them aside to tell them Dad's "final story."

My only regret was that he wasn't there to tell it himself. His delivery was always better than mine.

We never did figure out why the pacemaker started beeping then. But I have a hunch it was God granting him his last wish: one more story to tell.

I can picture it now.

Dad would be standing there before God, saying: "Aw, c'mon, let me make it beep just when they're all standing over the casket. Man, that'll be so funny. They'll be talking about it for years."

And God, who had gifted Dad with his fabulous sense of humor, would say, "Yeah, let's have some fun."

www.ingramcontent.com/pod-product-compliance
Lightning Source LLC
Chambersburg PA
CBHW042342300426
44109CB00048B/2672